Cheryl Frances-Hoad

LAST MAN STANDING

for baritone and orchestra

(2018)

Vocal Score

CHESTER

 Commissioned by BBC Radio 3 and first performed by Marcus Farnsworth and the BBC Symphony Orchestra conducted by Martyn Brabbins on 30th November 2018 at the Barbican, London.

Duration: *c.* 28 minutes

Vocal Score: CH88045-01
Study Score: CH88045-02
Parts are available on hire from the publisher.
www.musicsalesclassical.com

TEXT

I.

In Flanders fields

Where Poppies grow

Between the headstones,

Row on row,

I stumble through the scarlet snow

In search of friends I used to know.

Before my burning eyes,

A stolen generation lies

Of boys whose lives were thrown away

By those who played

At genocide

And burned the world to ash

For pride.

And as I wander to and fro,

Around my feet

The poppies blow.

II.

Poppies.

Bloodstained.

Black-hearted.

Blasted from the

Battered earth.

Roots writhing

Through the bones

Of broken men.

Each bloom a wound,

Torn round a sooty core.

The blazing echo of a shot.

A flaming red forget-me-not.

III.

The day we enlisted,

My pals and I,

The sun smiled

In a cloudless sky.

We marched away to fight the Hun

With flags and banners,

Trumpet, drum.

Lads who meant the world to me;

Cooper HP, White KT,

Evans AG, Clarke JO –

Ginger, Chalky, Taff and Joe.

Hearts proud, heads high,

Joining in the battle cry:

'God for Empire, England

And King George'.

And the Band played 'Tipperary'

As the soldiers waved goodbye.

We'd have the Kaiser on the run

Before the year was done,

And then return.

Well, we were young

And we would learn.

IV.

Training camp,

A no-man's land.

Men herded in from far and wide:

Tinkers, tailors,

Soldiers, sailors,

Rich men, poor men, side by side.

Form fours, right turn.

Clean your boots and shine your brass.

Learn to shoot and march in time.

Kiss the colonel on his a – (rse).

Watson RF, Taylor B,

Green AR and Richards P,

Answering our country's call.

All for one and one for all.

V.

To France at last

To do our part,

Mustard-keen to make a start.

Tramping mile on endless mile -

Hoist your packs

And smile, boys, smile -

On through green and pleasant lands,

The fate of nations in our hands.

But as we near the battlefields,

The rolling landscape yields

To regions wrecked by shot and shell -

A world that war has blown to hell.

VI.

An earthen ocean,

Floods the horizon.

The pearls and corals

In its shell-strewn pools

Not gems,

But scattered teeth and bones

Of nameless soldiers

Come to dust.

Charred tree stumps

Point towards the skies,

Their birdless branches

Mute beneath the thundering guns.

Fierce forests of ferocious wire

Grasp their flapping prey.

The setting sun incarnadines the land,

As though the soil itself were weeping blood.

It is not

Nor it cannot come

To good.

VII.

A rude awakening

From foolish dreams of glory.

No Camelot lies waiting here

Amid the death and grief and fear,

Where every man must take his chance,

Fall in and join the fatal dance.

And the days pass,

And the weeks pass

And there's nothing to do

But sit on your arse

And fire at the whites of Jerry's eyes

And live with the stink

And the mud and the flies.

And each day,

A little bit more of you

Dies.

VIII.

A timeless, twilight world,

Smoke-choked,

Rain-soaked,

Where rats

As big as cats grow fat

On the flesh

Of fallen friends,

And lice feast on the sluggish blood

Of those men left alive.

Eyes that sparkled yesterday

Stare sightless from

Bomb-blasted holes.

Trench walls run with blood.

The flash of shellfire

And the hungry roar of guns

Blur day and night to one.

And this is hell,

And we are here.

[Because we're here

Because we're here

Because we're here...]

IX.

At last,

The long-awaited news.

A massed attack along the front

To end this state

Of stalemate

And win the war.

Old hands shrug -

They've heard it all before -

But Johnny Raws are mad

To show our stuff.

Our day of reckoning

Can't come soon enough.

X.

Dawn light
Slides across the trench.
The air is thick
With cigarettes
And petrol-tainted tea.
The guns have fallen silent
And in the unfamiliar quiet
I can hear
A blackbird singing
Somewhere near.
My senses sharp in the morning air,
I am aware
Of every little movement in the ranks.
A sergeant coughs.
The rum can clanks.
Men smoke, and joke,
And pray, and cry,
And steel themselves to do or die.
Then Zero hour,
Whistles blow,
And over the top
The Tommies go...
Right lads - CHARGE!
God Save the King!

XI.

Over the Top (Orchestral)

XII.

Hello?
Hello?
Ginger? Joe?
Chalky? Taff?
Somebody
Answer me!
Watson? Taylor?
Richards? Green?
Can anybody hear?
Is anybody there?
Lads? Lads?
Hello?
Oh, Please, God
No...

XIII.

I cannot speak
Of what I saw
When we were ordered
To withdraw.
Of the countless men
In that attack,
Pitifully few came back.
Chalky, Ginger, Taff and Joe -
Wiped out at a single blow.
Watson, Richards, Taylor, Green,
Unrecongnisable,
Obscene.
Rank on rank
Shelled and shot,
And for what?
For what?

XIV.

Next day

It begins again.

As up the line march

More young men,

Replacing those

Who've gone before -

Fresh meat to feed

This bloody war.

And so it will go

On and on,

Until at last

The job is done.

XV.

In Flanders fields

Where Poppies grow

Between the headstones,

Row on row,

A blackbird sings from nearby trees

As they dance gently in the breeze.

I kept my word,

I came to find

The fallen friends I left behind.

Now I know where they lie.

I've said my last goodbye.

And as I turn away to go,

Around my feet

The poppies blow.

Tamsin Collison

Last Man Standing

TAMSIN COLLISON

CHERYL FRANCES-HOAD

Copyright © Chester Music 2018

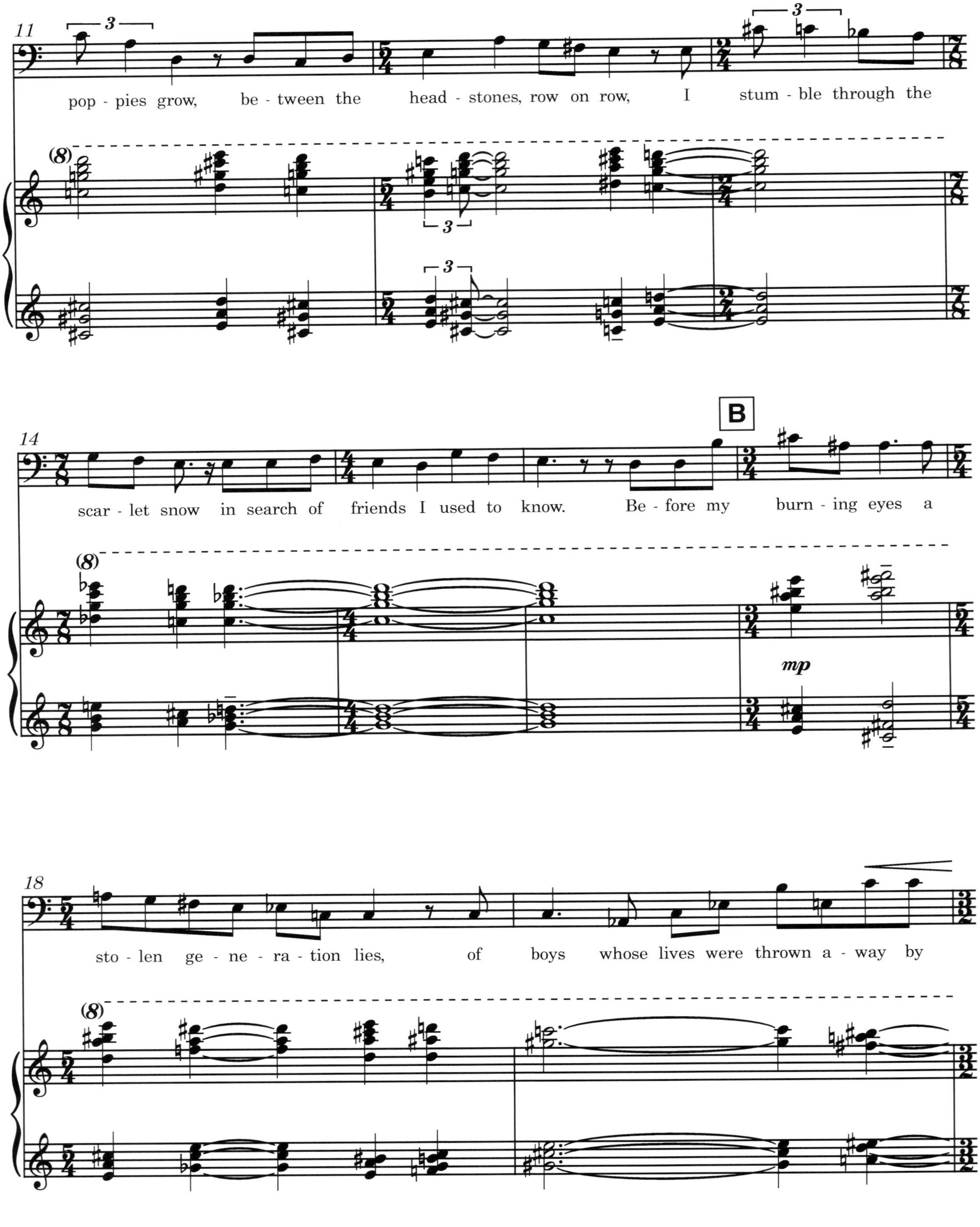
11
pop - pies grow, be - tween the head - stones, row on row, I stum - ble through the
14
scar - let snow in search of friends I used to know. Be - fore my burn - ing eyes a
B
mp
18
sto - len ge - ne - ra - tion lies, of boys whose lives were thrown a - way by

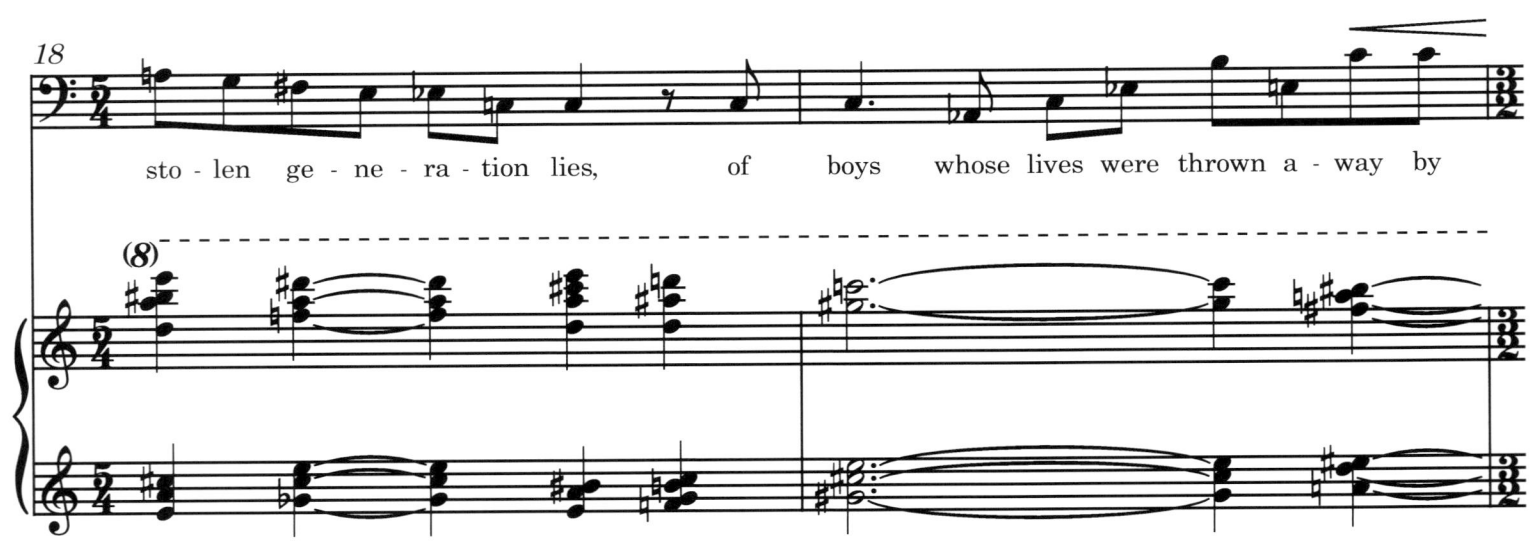

20
più f
f
those who played at ge - no - cide and burned the world to ash for
(8)
loco
mf
Ped.
23
mf
pride. And as I wan - der to and fro, a - round my
loco
(Ped.)
26
3
feet the pop - pies blow.
p
(Ped.)
6
7

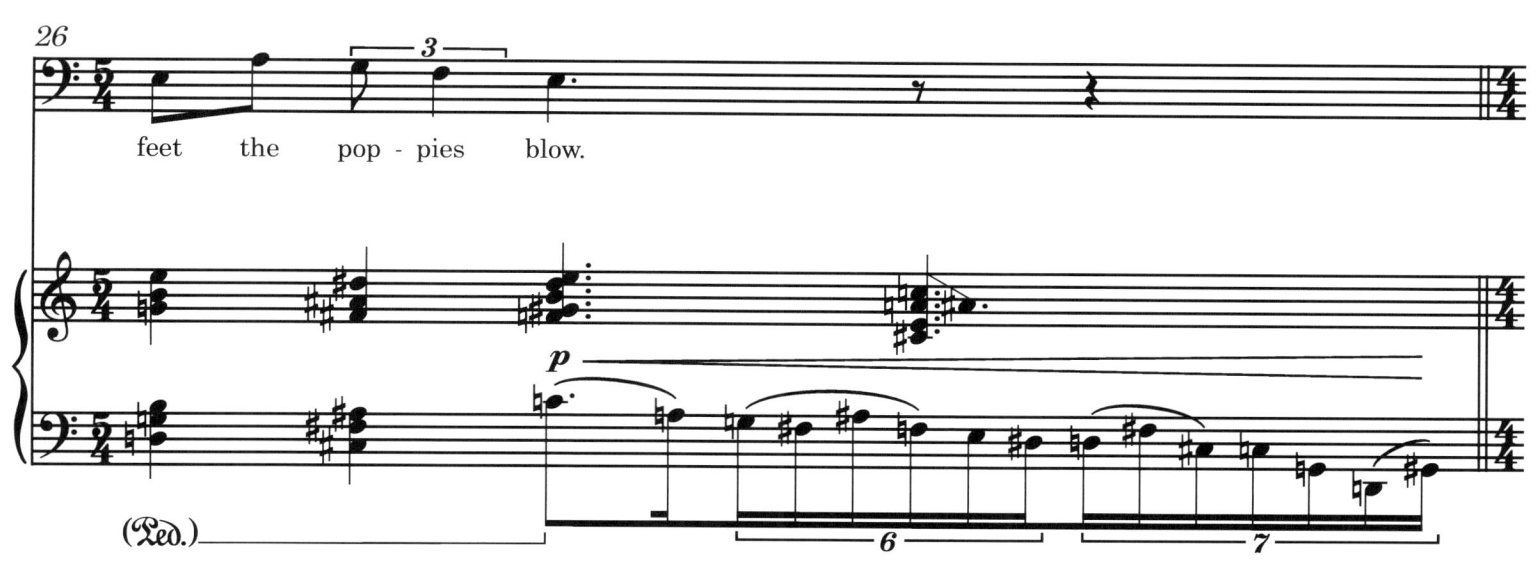

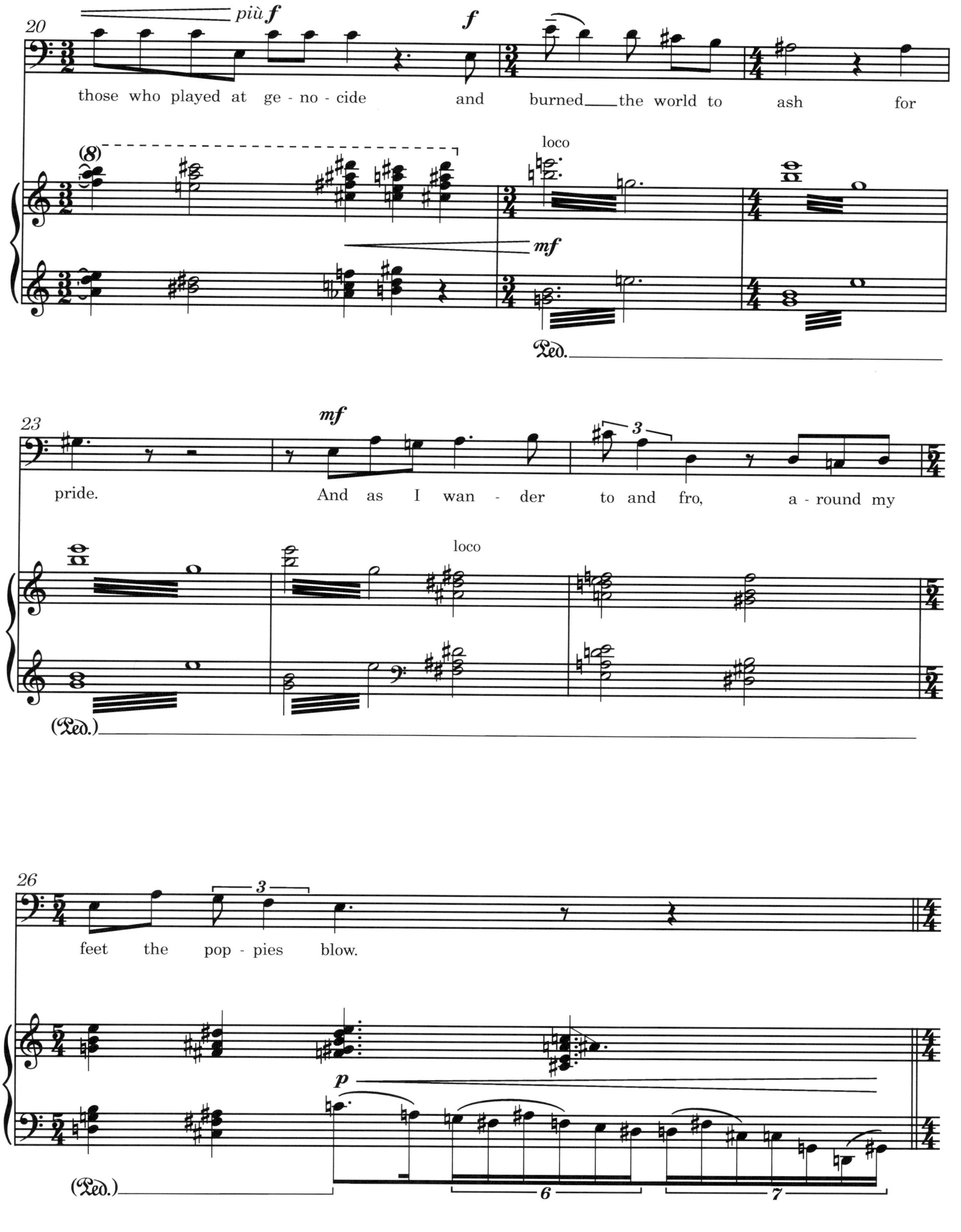

When this bloody war is over, Oh, how happy I will be;
When I get my civvy clothes on, No more soldiering for me.
(What a friend we have in Jesus! All our sins and griefs to bear!
What a privilege to carry, every thing to God in prayer.)

Last Man Standing

7

The Bells of Hell go ting-a-ling-a-ling, For you but not for me:
For me the angels sing-a-ling-a-ling, They've got the goods for me.

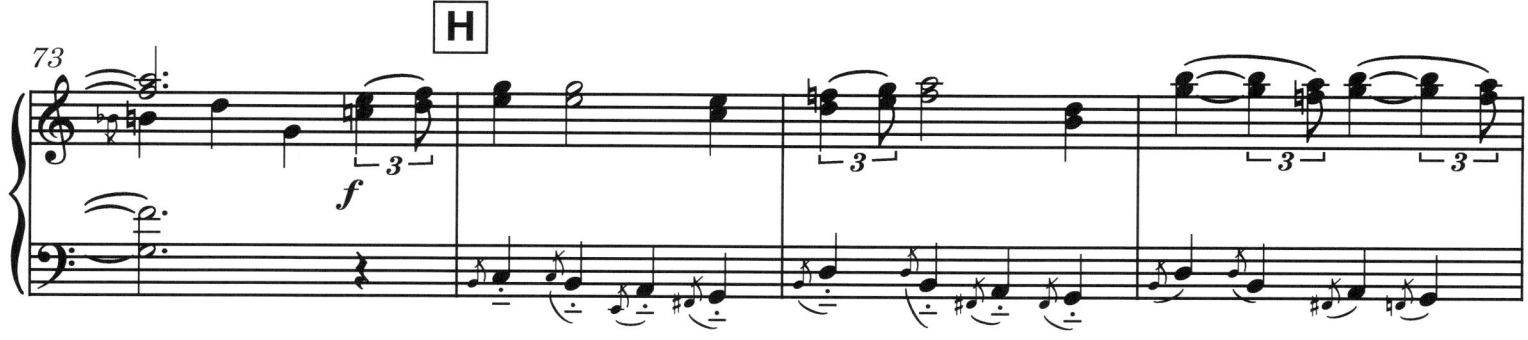

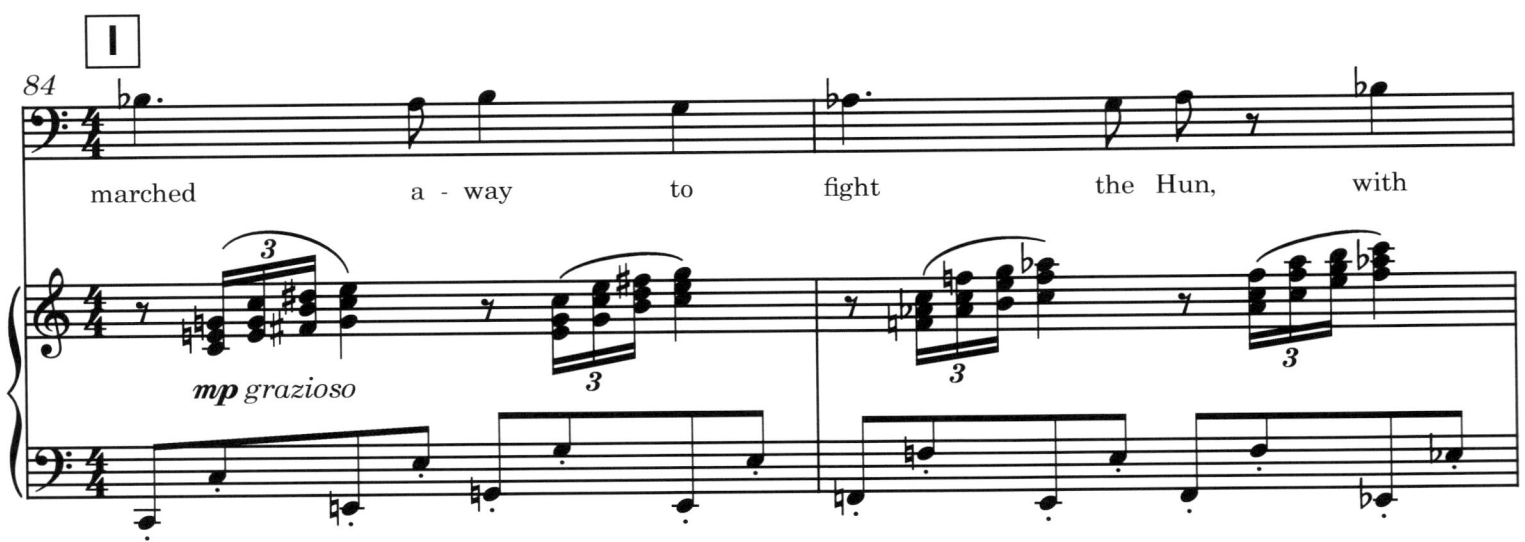

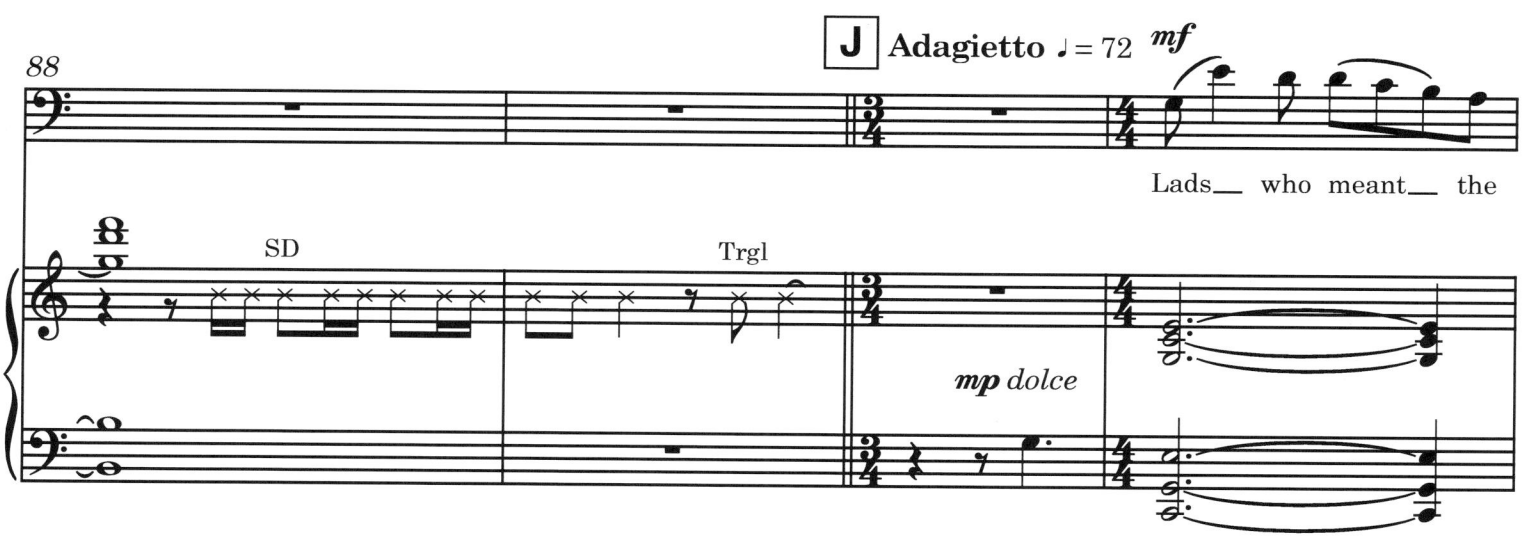
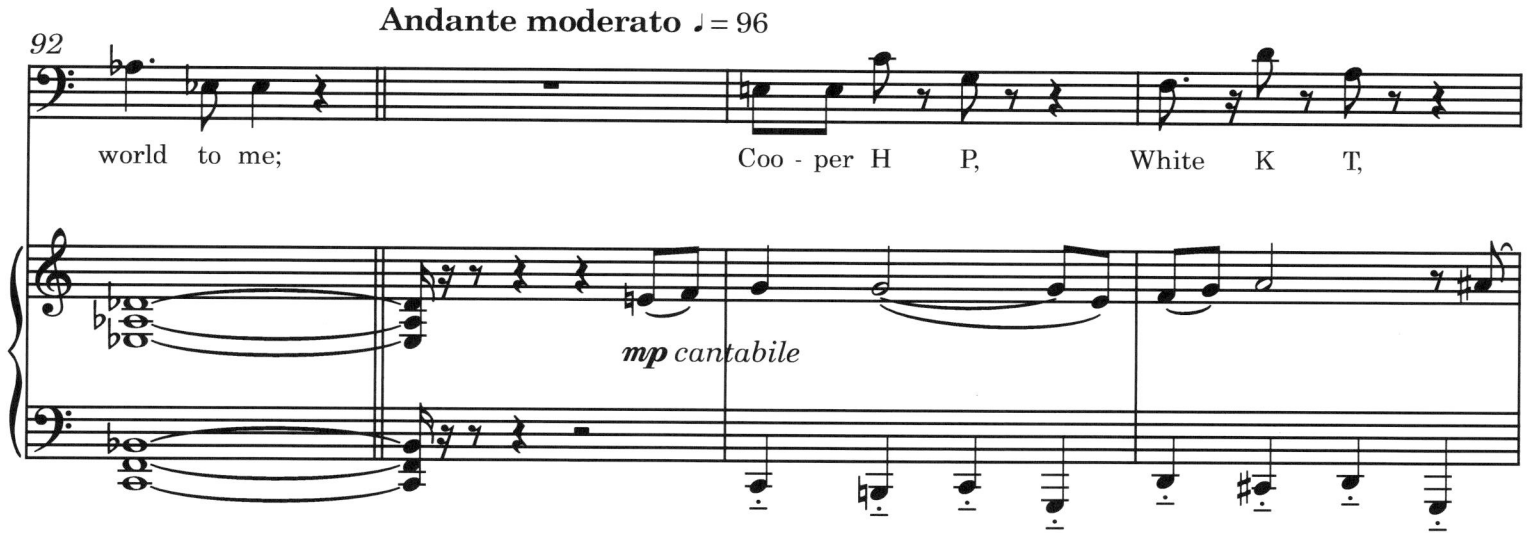
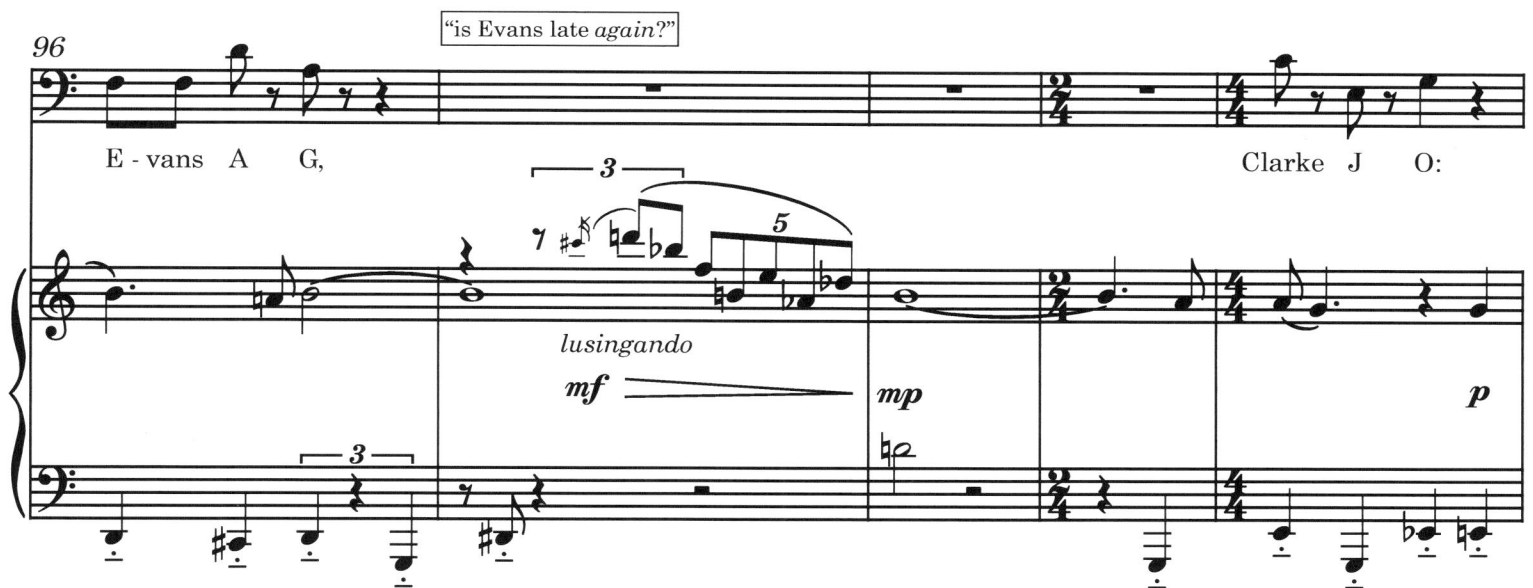

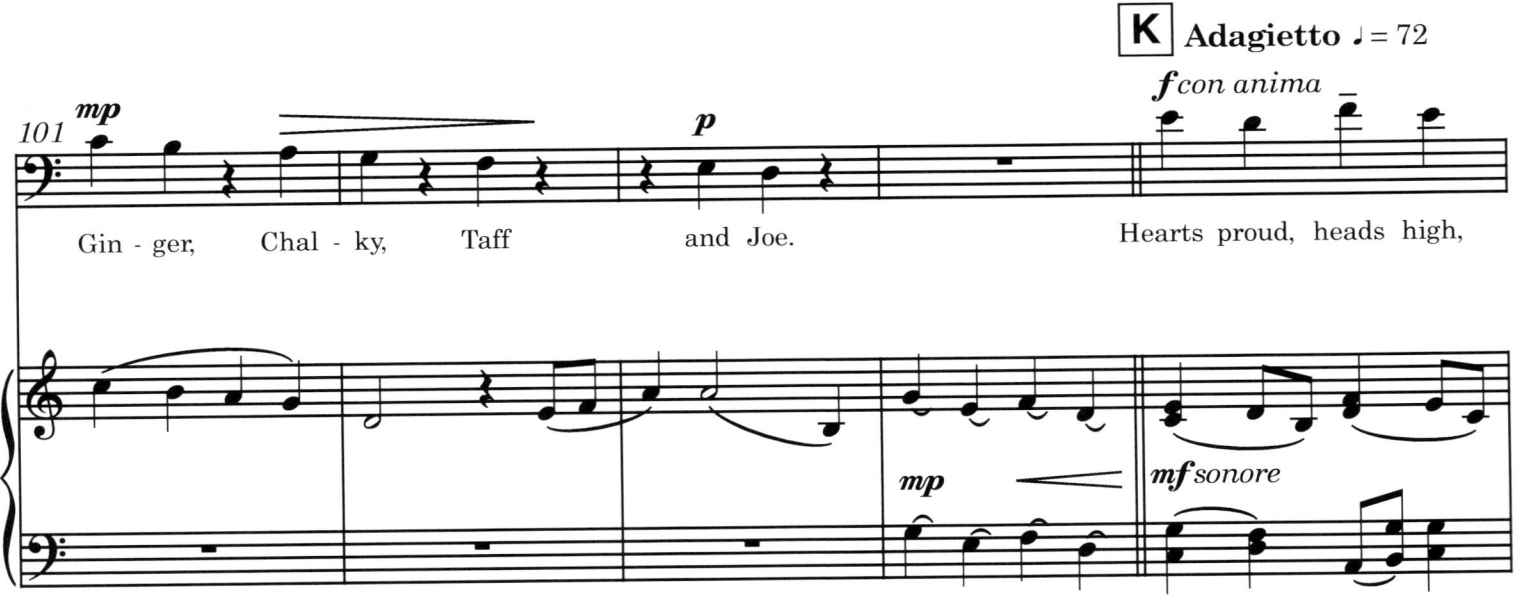
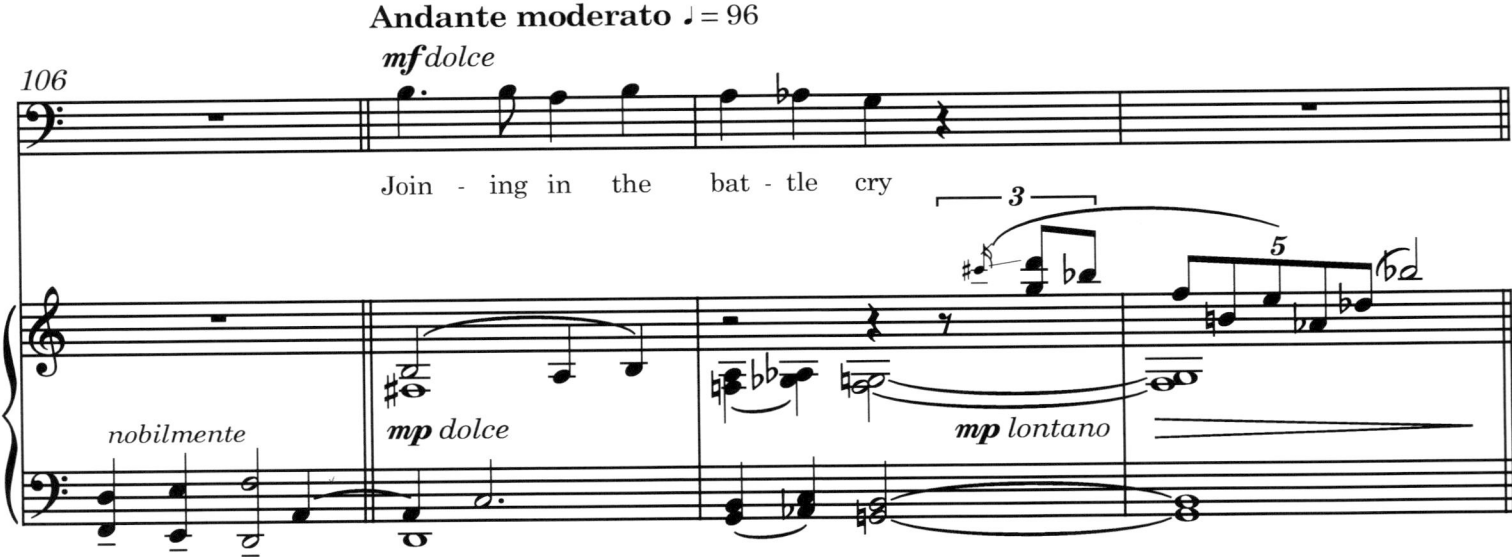
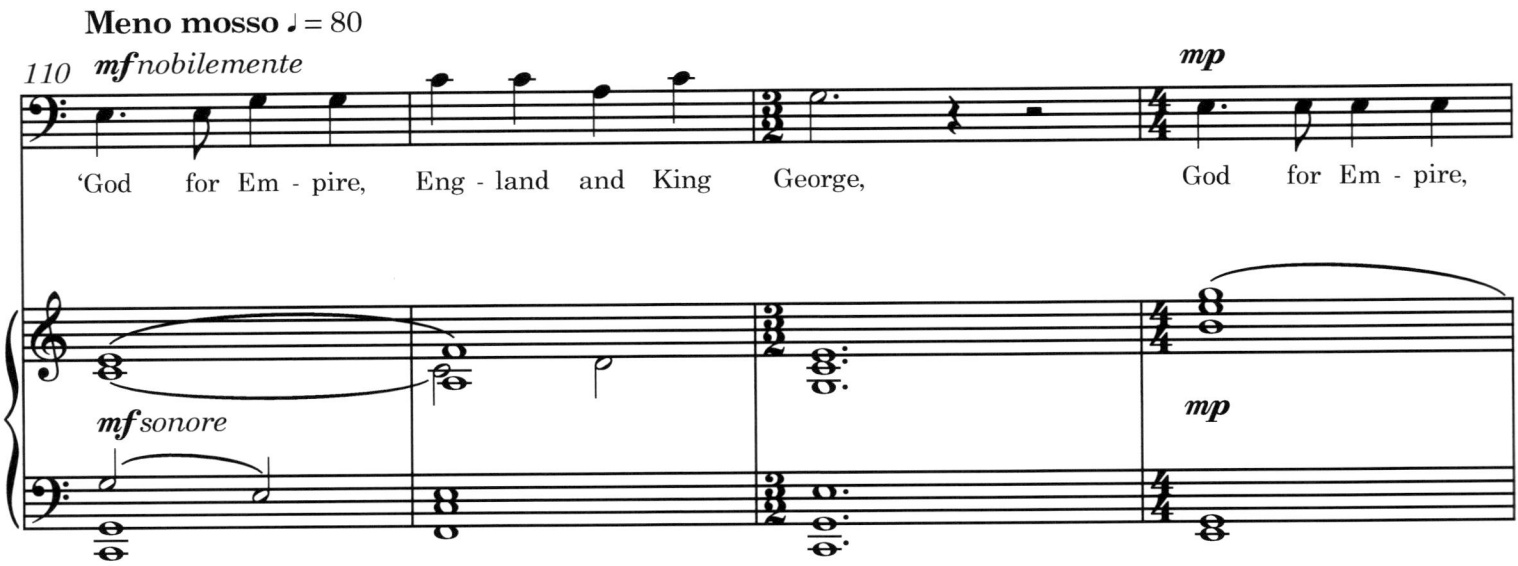

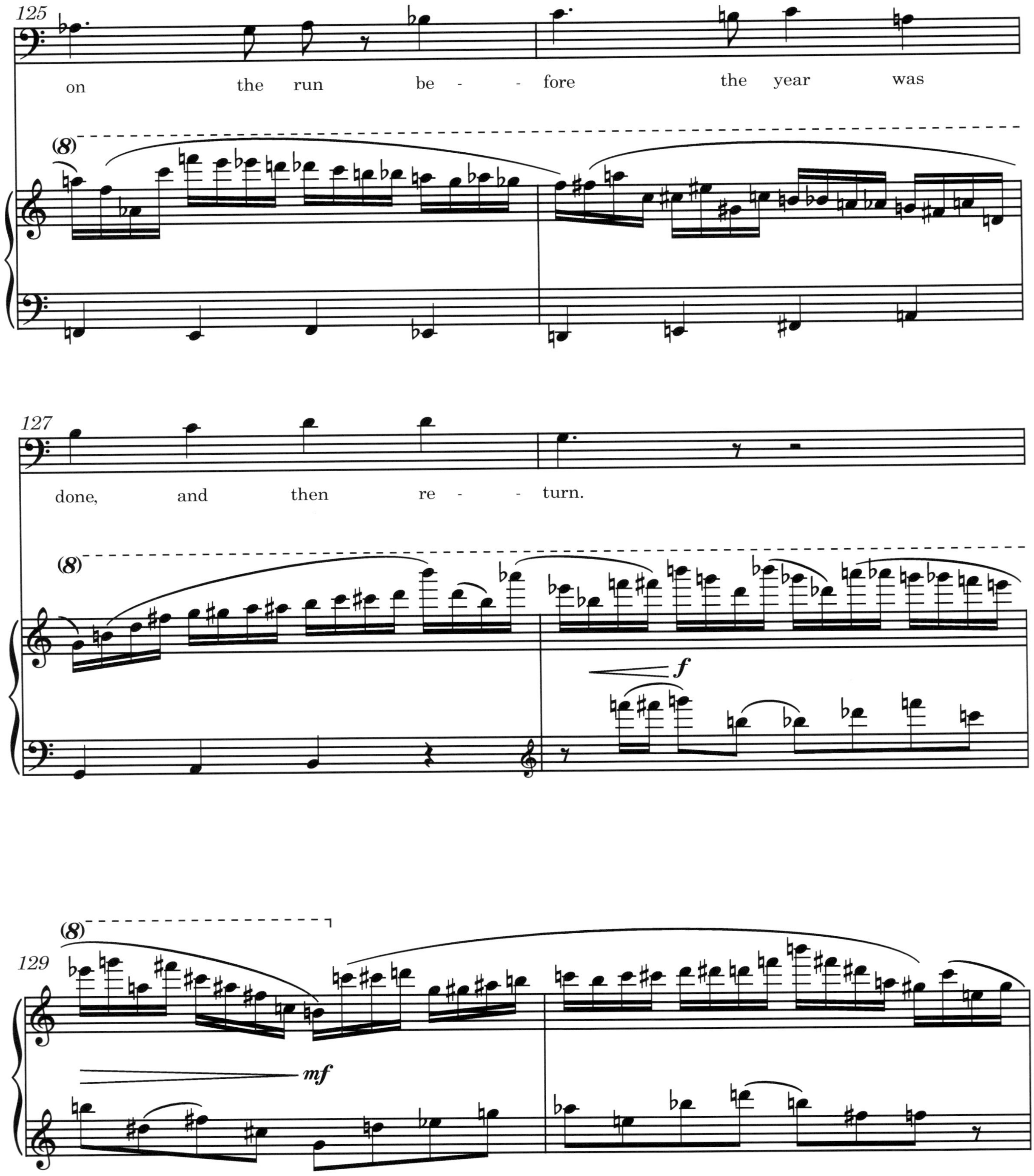
125
on the run be - - fore the year was
(8)
127
done, and then re - - turn.
(8)
f
(8)
129
mf

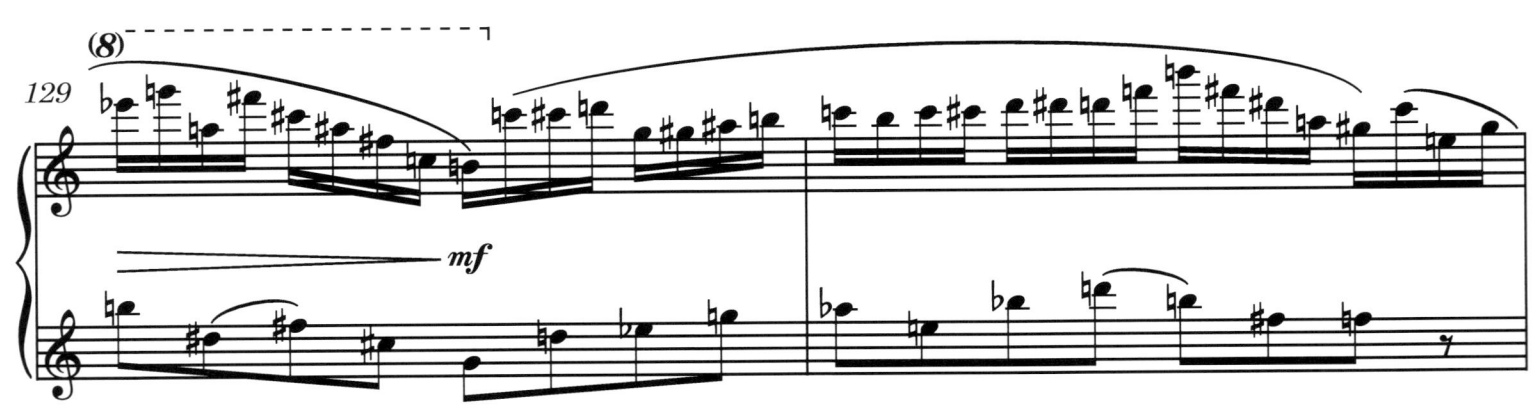

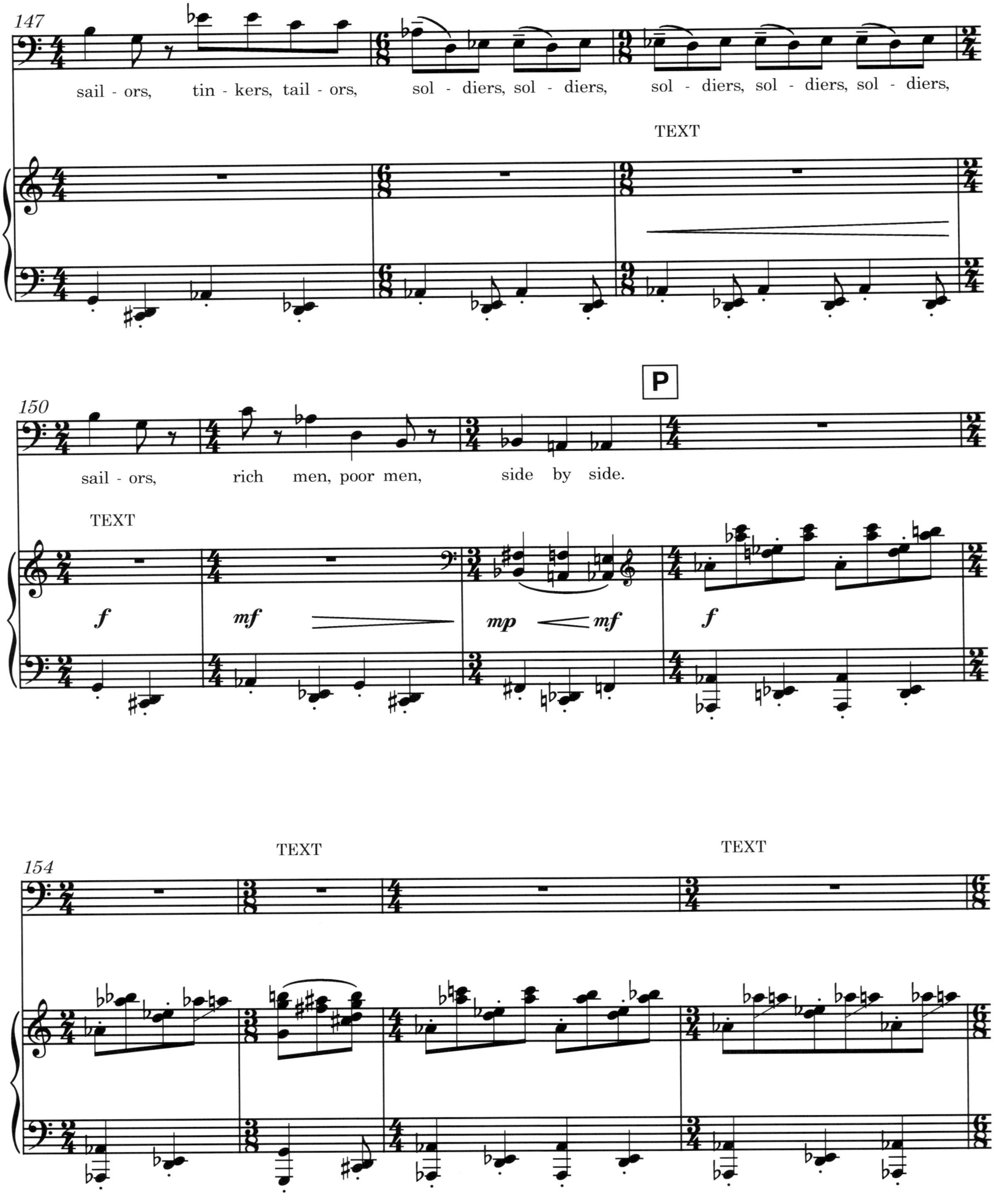
147
sail - ors, tin - kers, tail - ors, sol - diers, sol - diers, sol - diers, sol - diers, sol - diers,
TEXT
150
sail - ors, rich men, poor men, side by side.
P
TEXT
f
mf
mp
mf
f
154
TEXT
TEXT

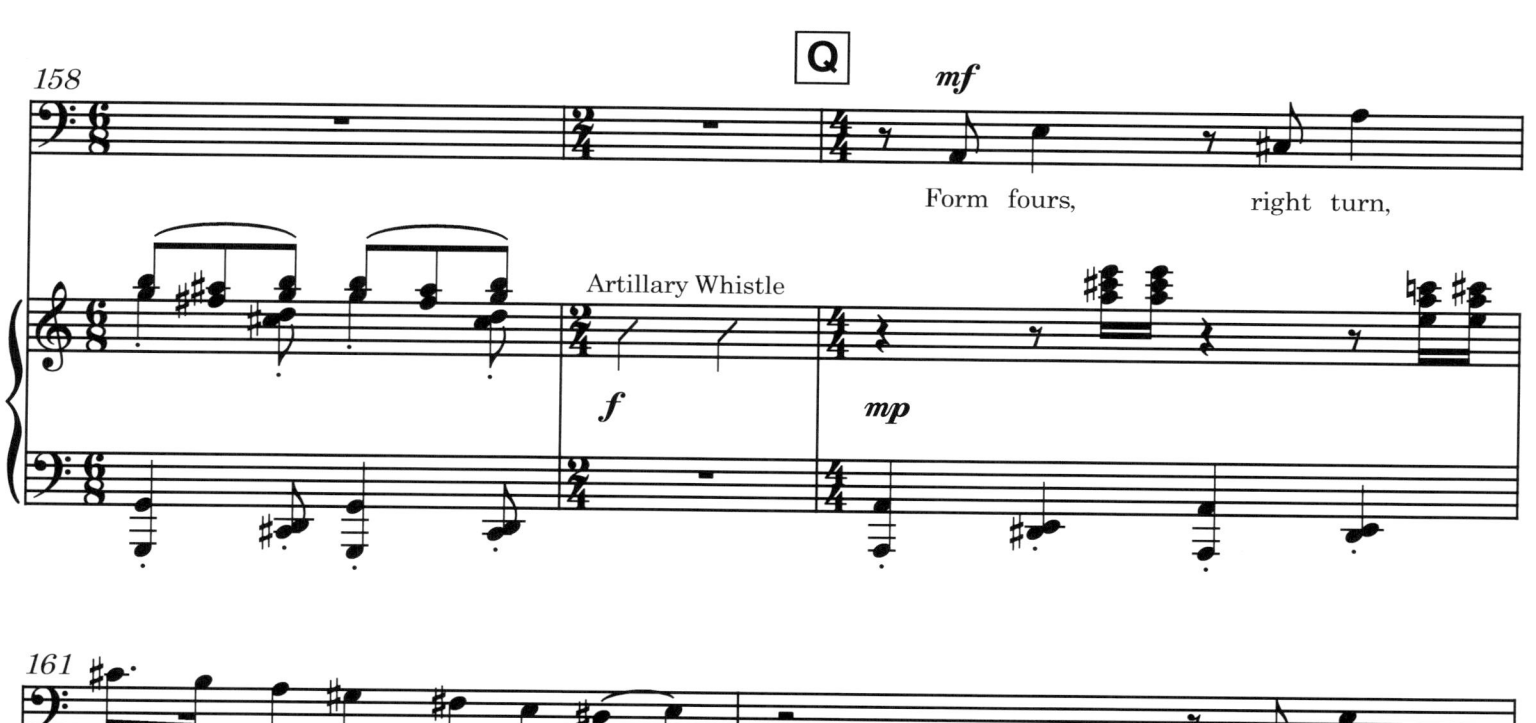

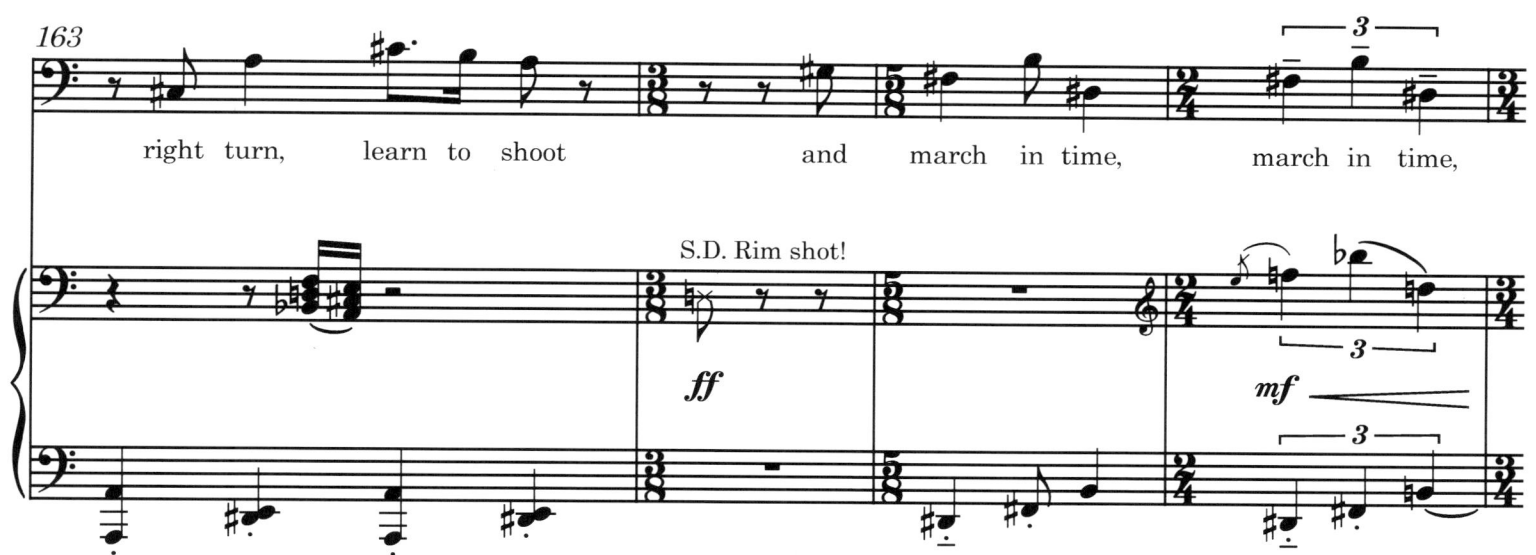

20
Last Man Standing

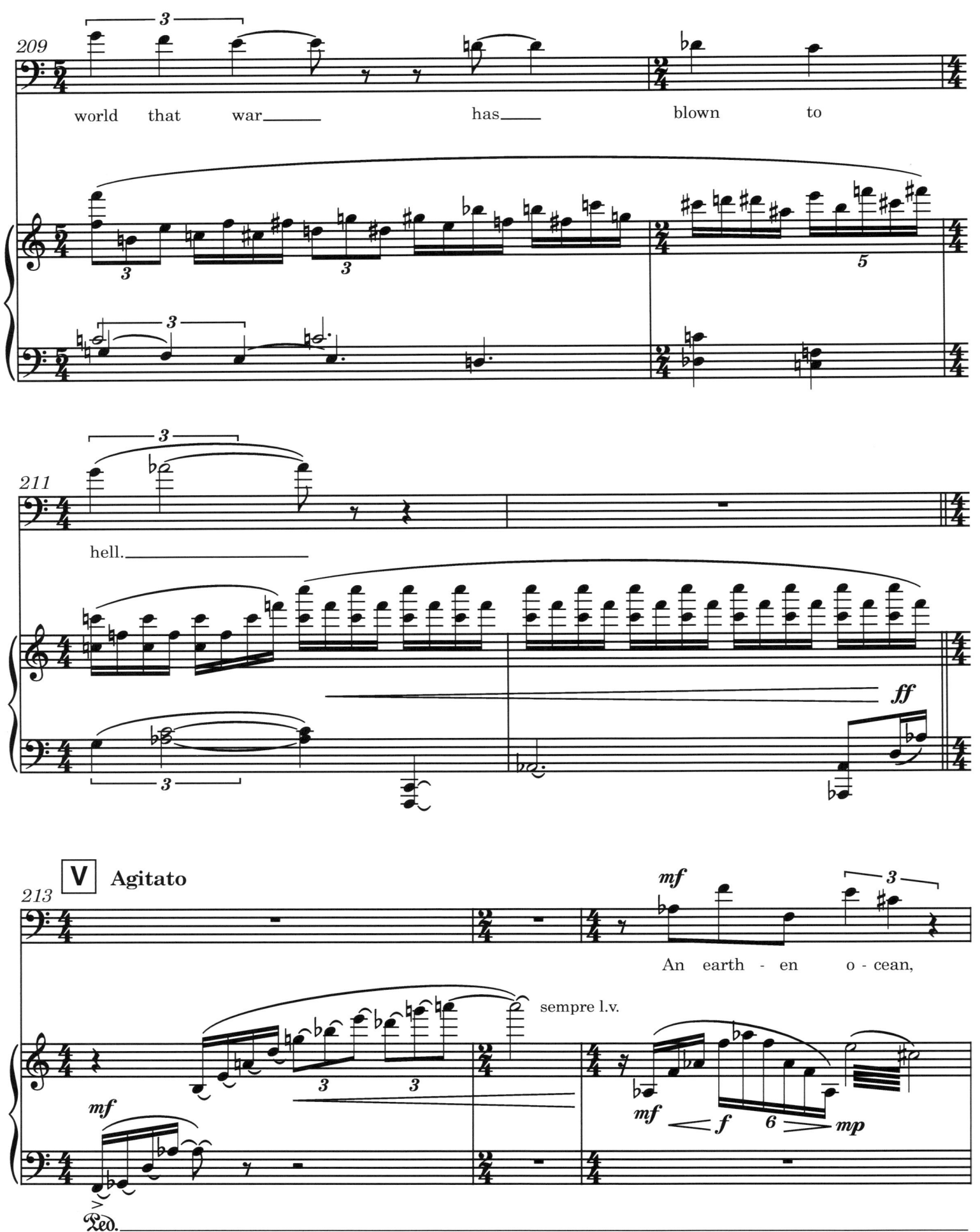

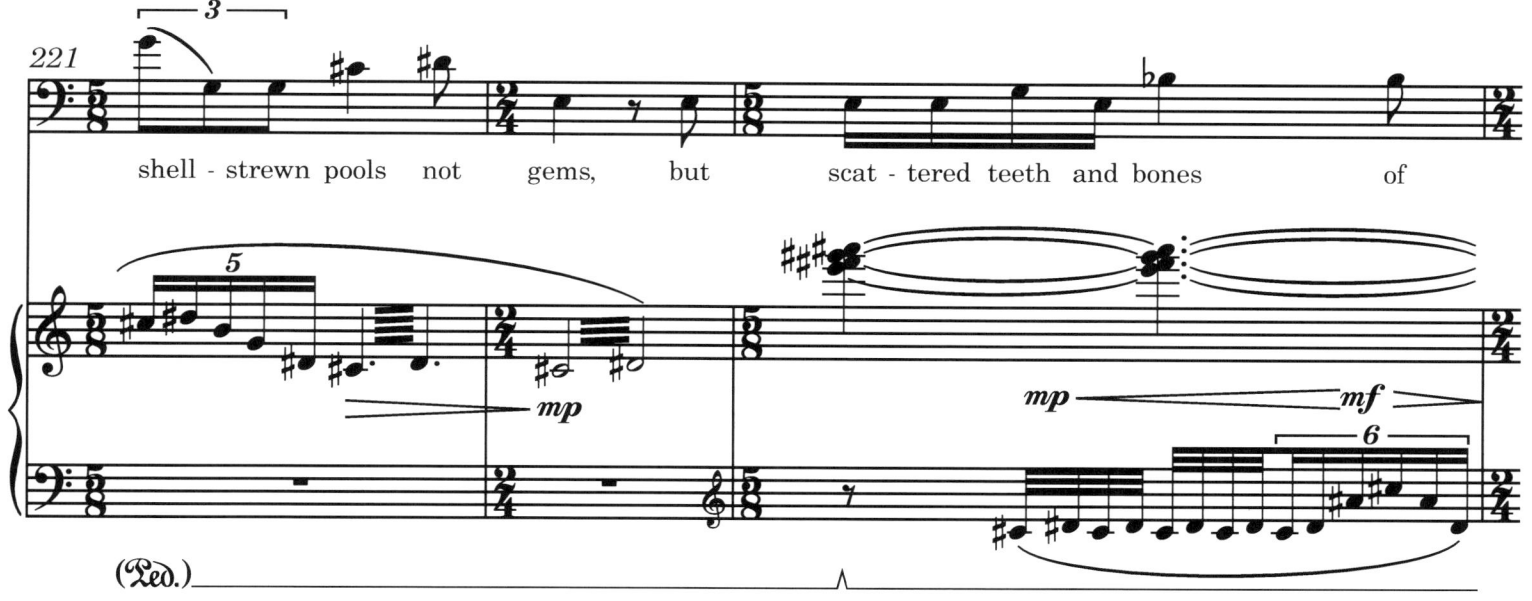

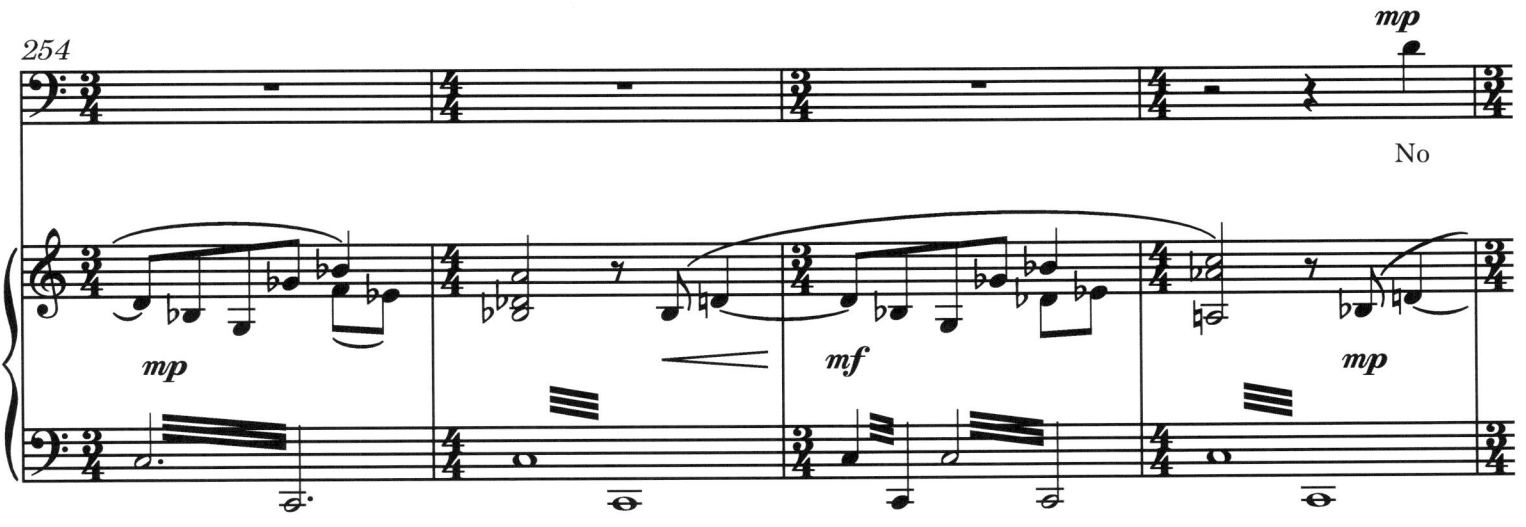

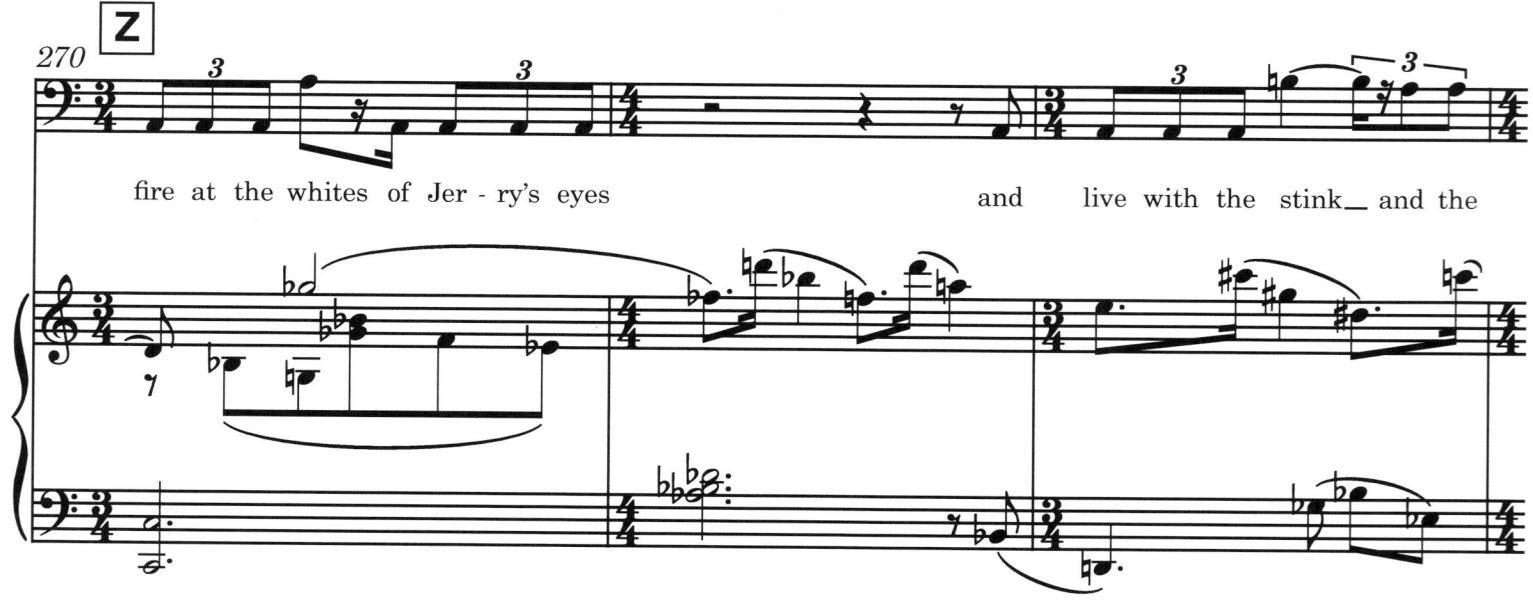

34 Last Man Standing

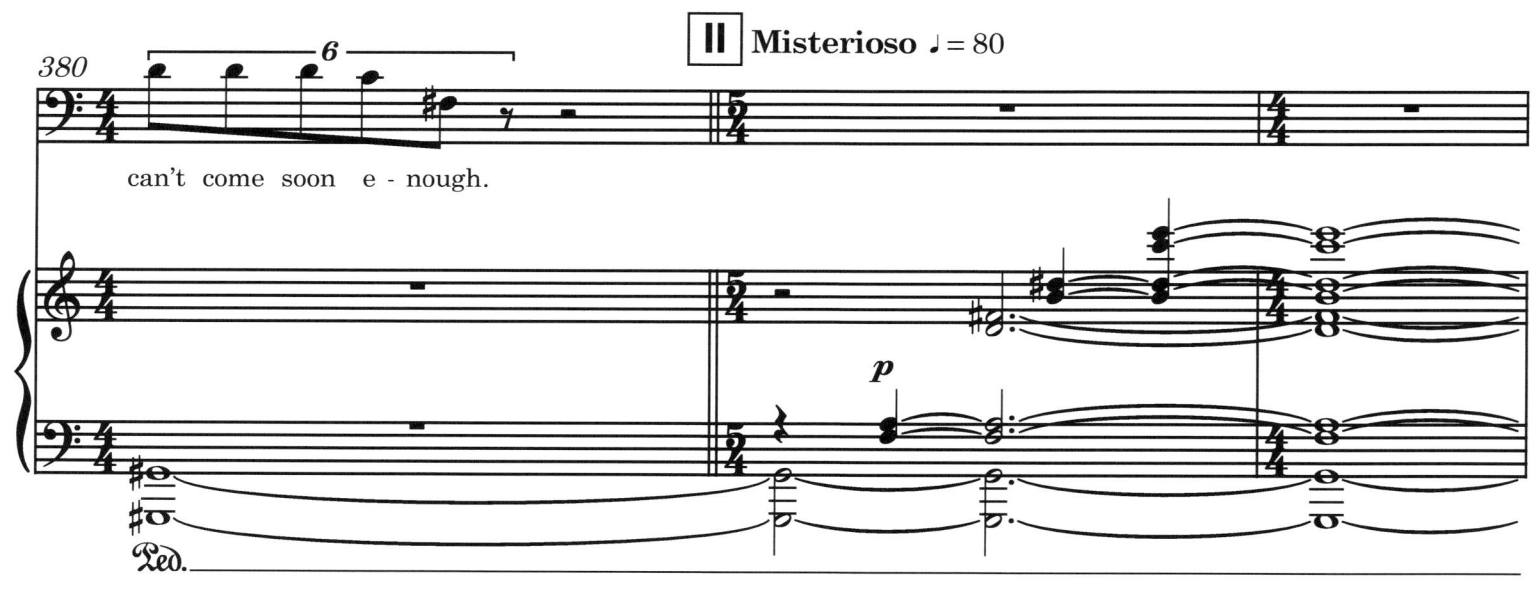

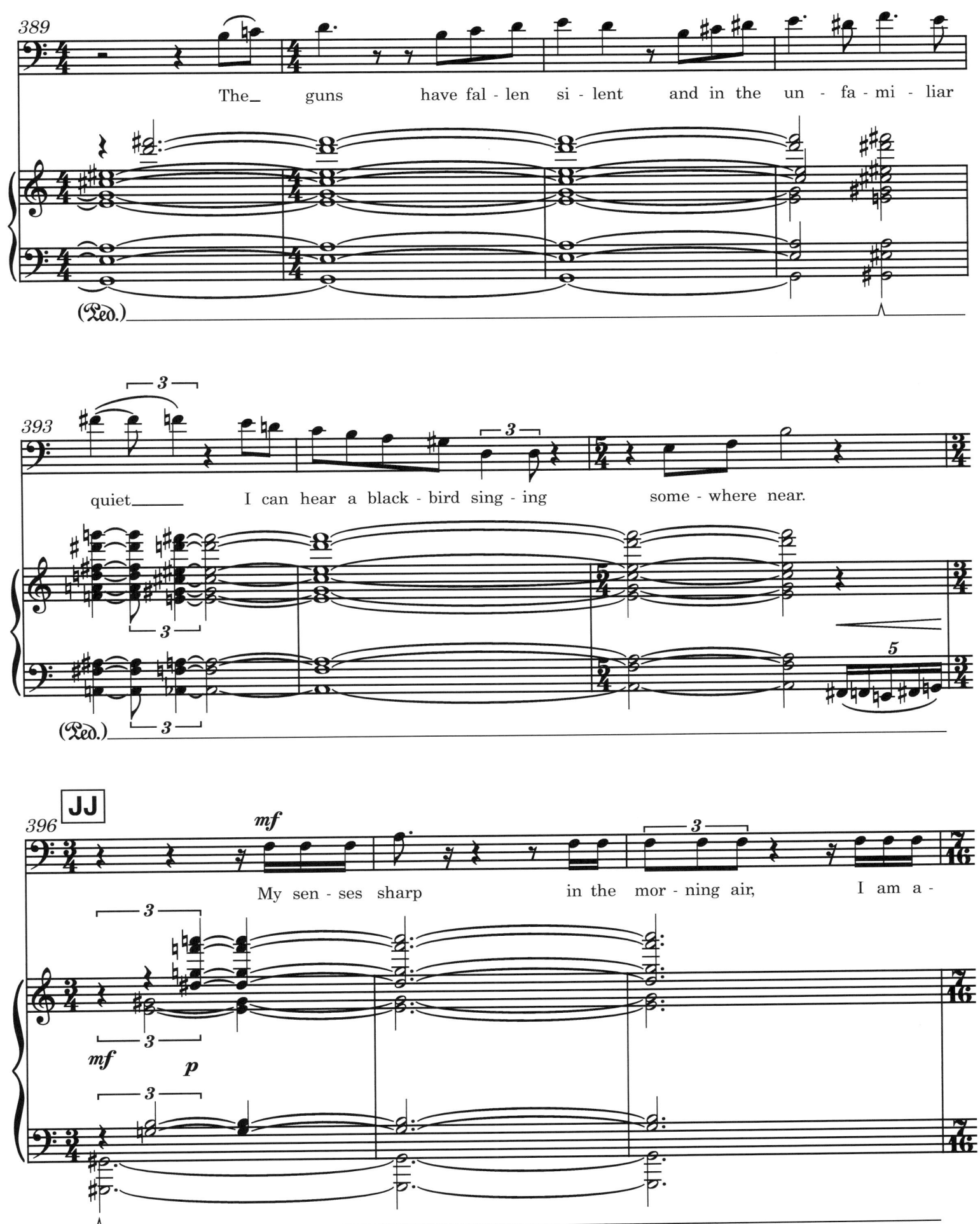

Last Man Standing

39

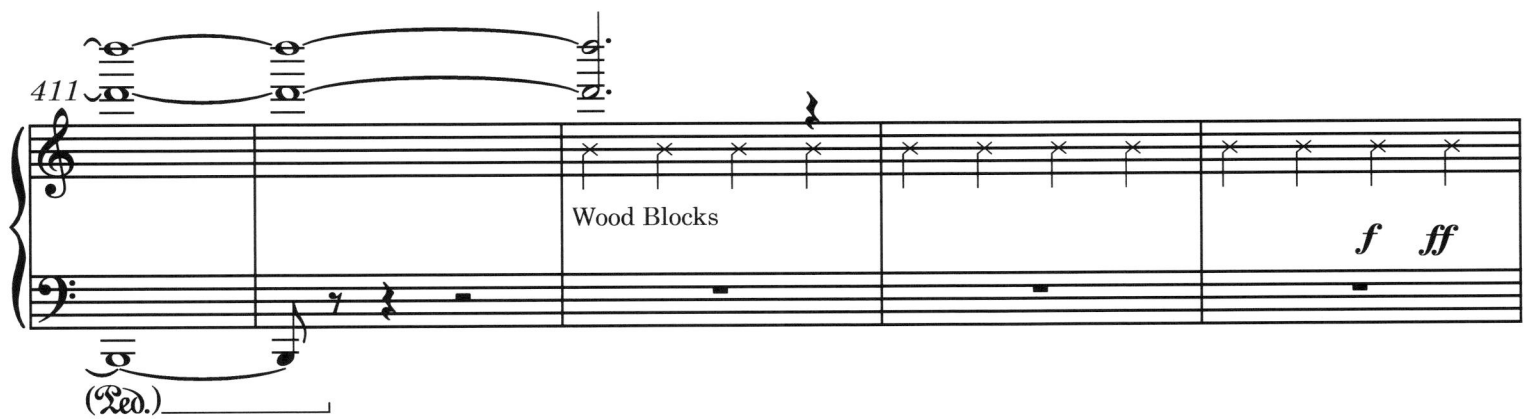

KK **Con fuoco (Allegro moderato)** (♩ = 120)

Then Zero hour, Whistles blow,
And over the top the Tommies go…

(Shouts)
Right lads - God save
CHARGE! the King!

Last Man Standing

LL *'My Lord the Gun! He lives in a lair that takes a month to build...an army toil to feed him with long rows of glistening shells. Men and gun are one and indivisible. My Lord the Gun has come into his own, and his kindom today is large - it is the world.'*
Lieutenant Adrian Consett-Stephen.

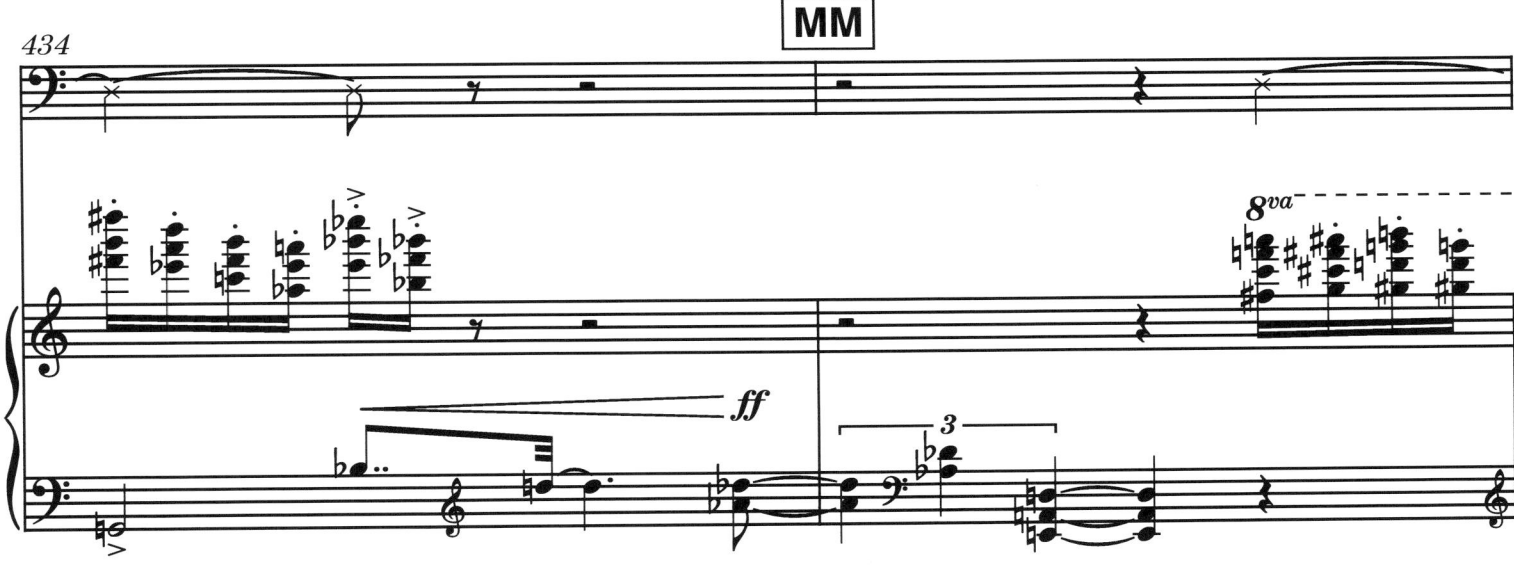

Last Man Standing

NN

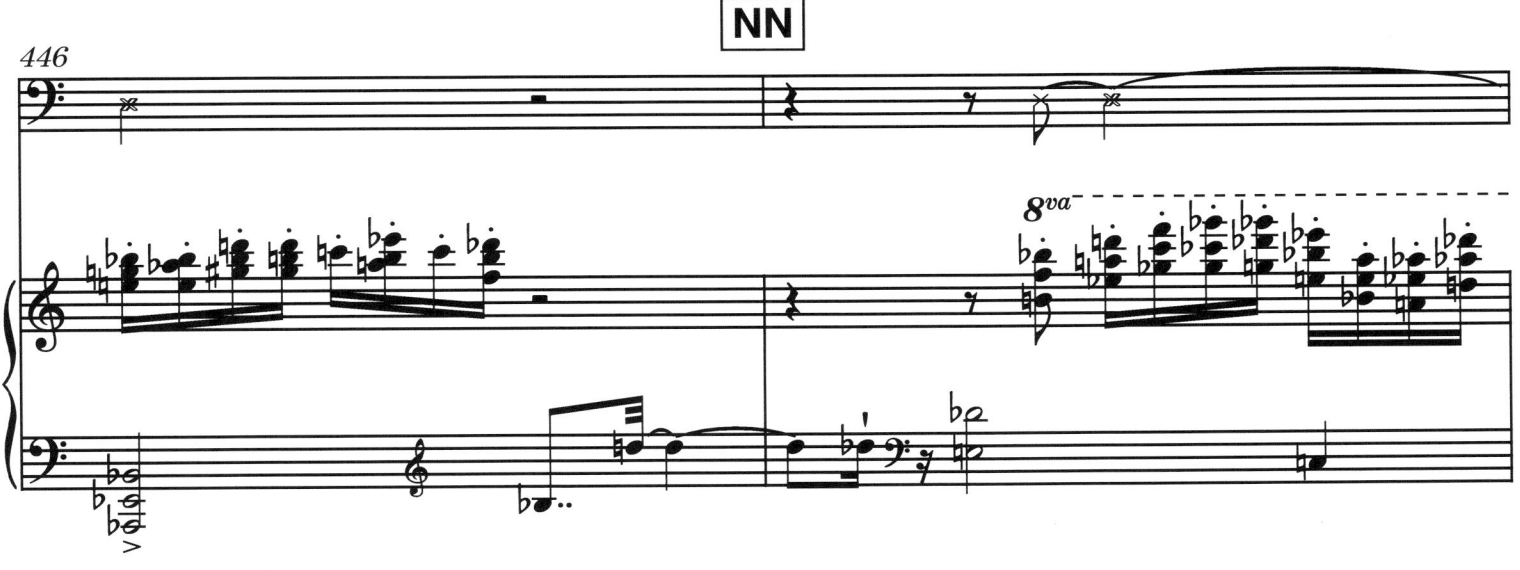
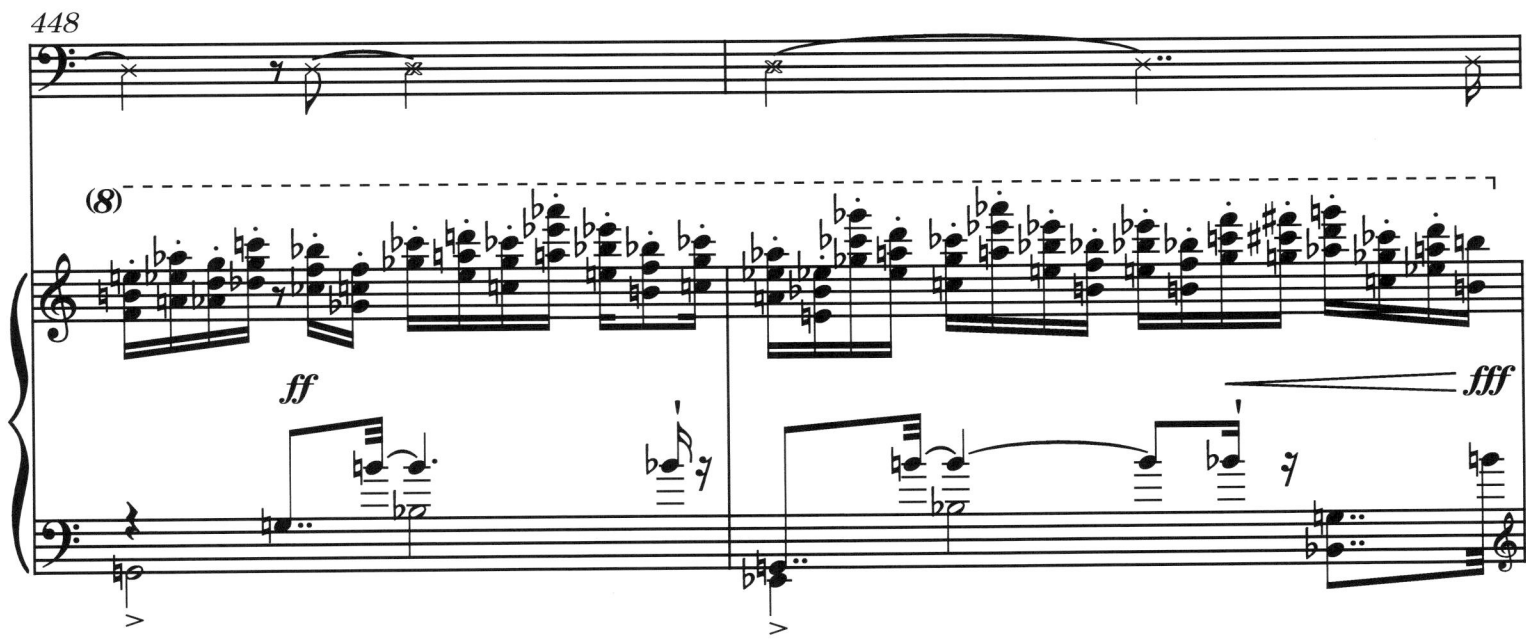
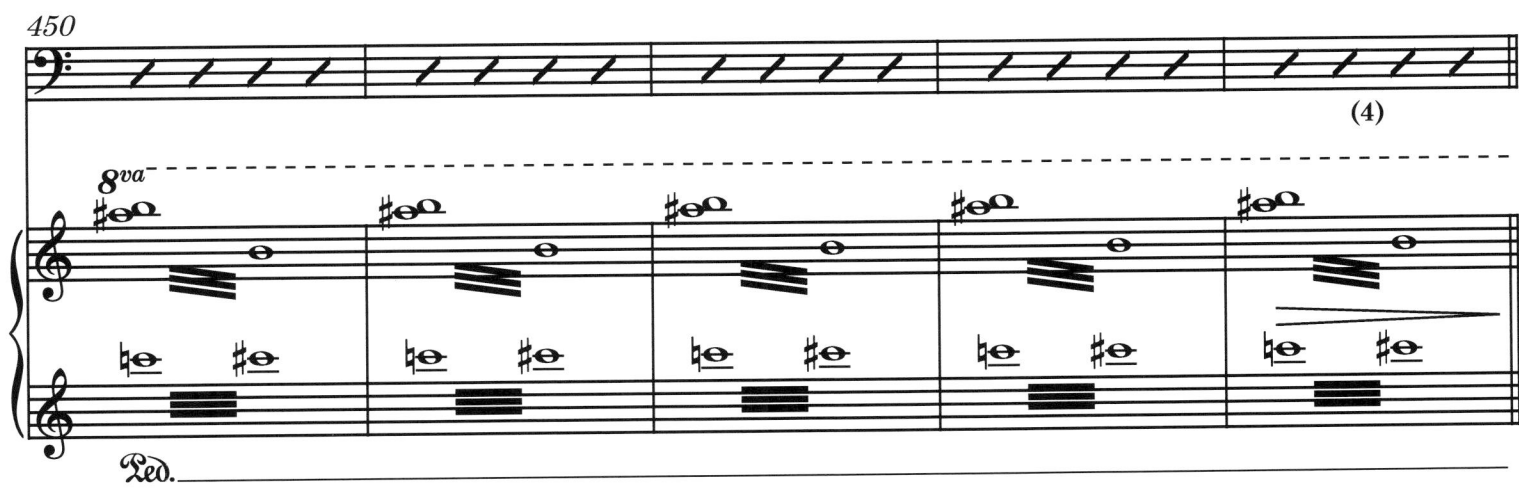

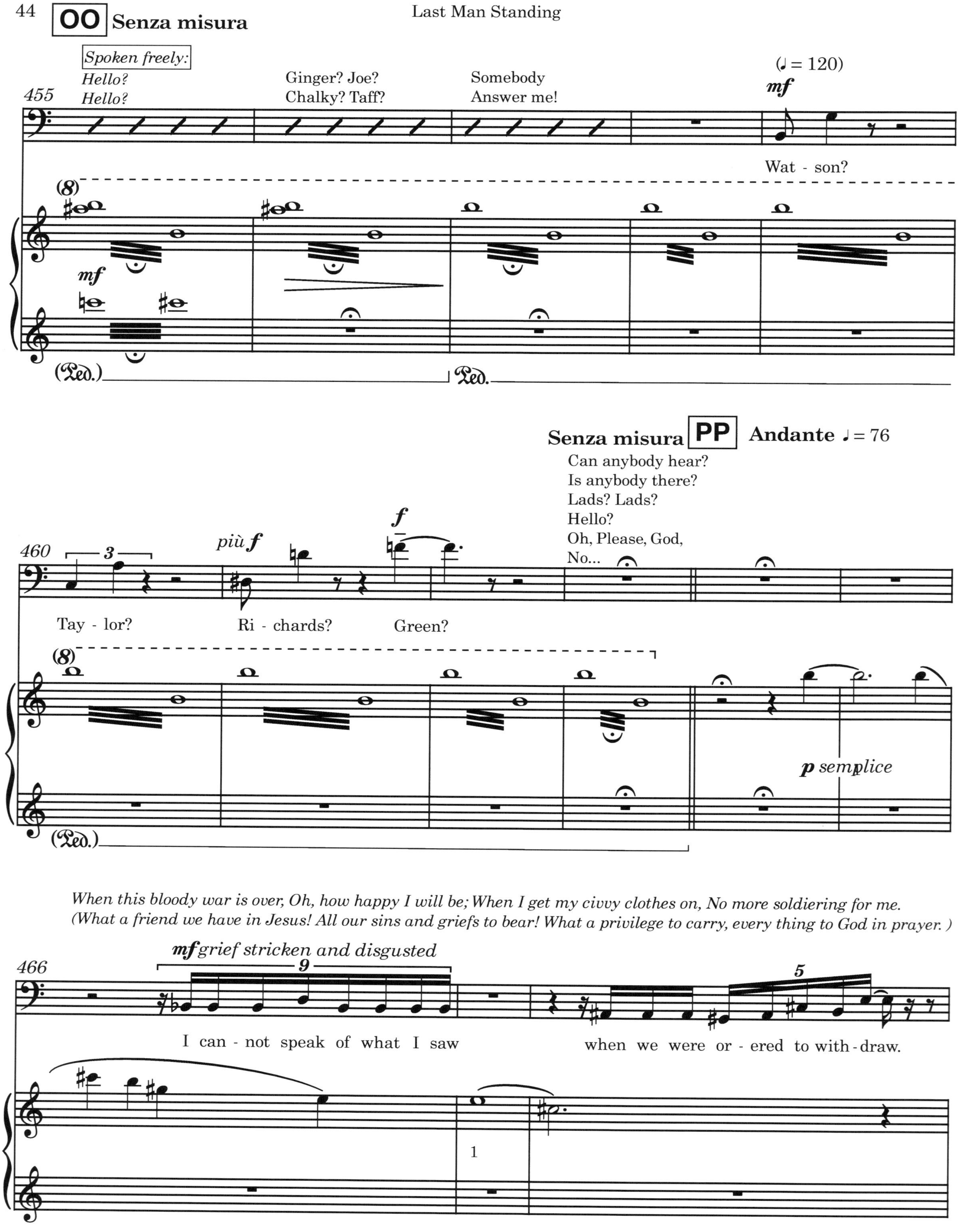

44 **OO** Senza misura Last Man Standing

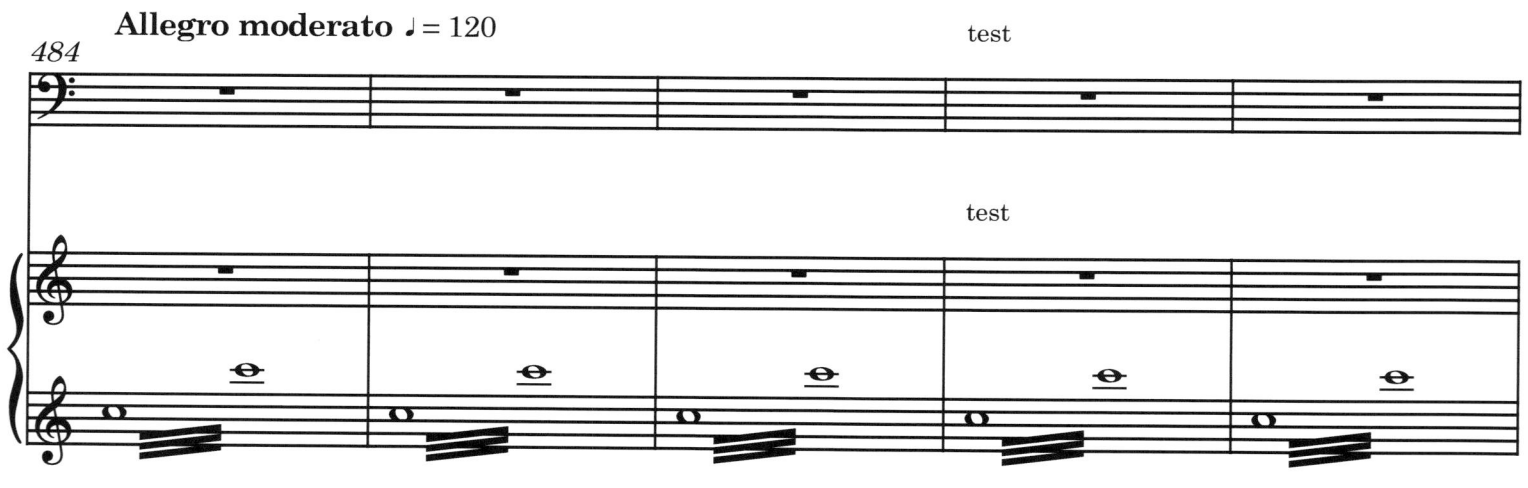

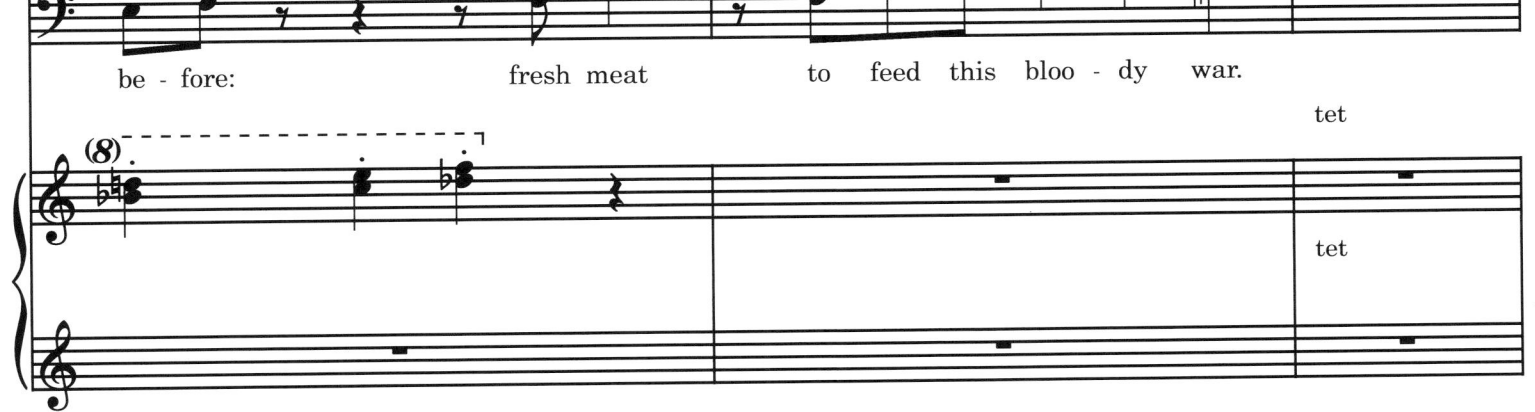

48 — Last Man Standing

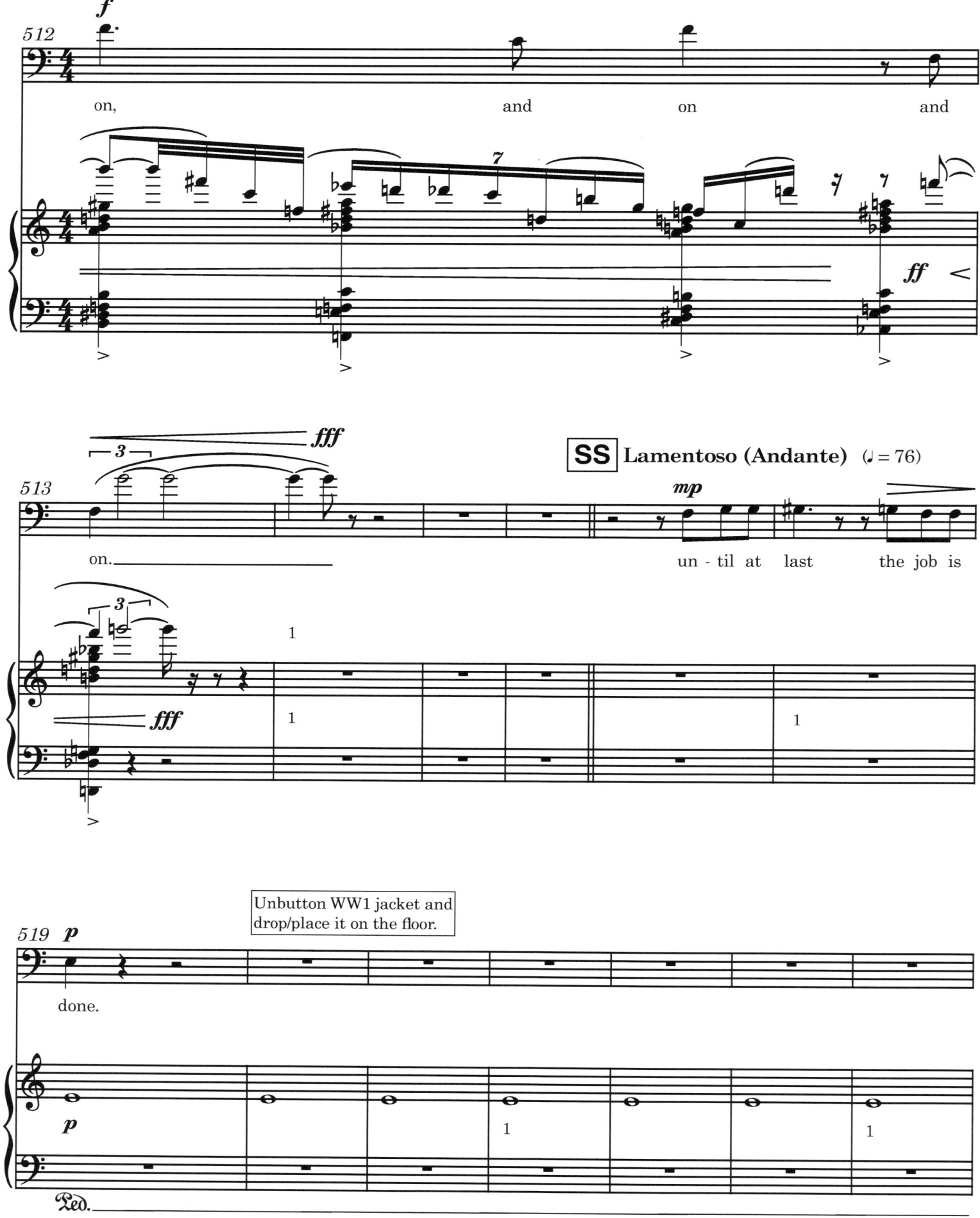

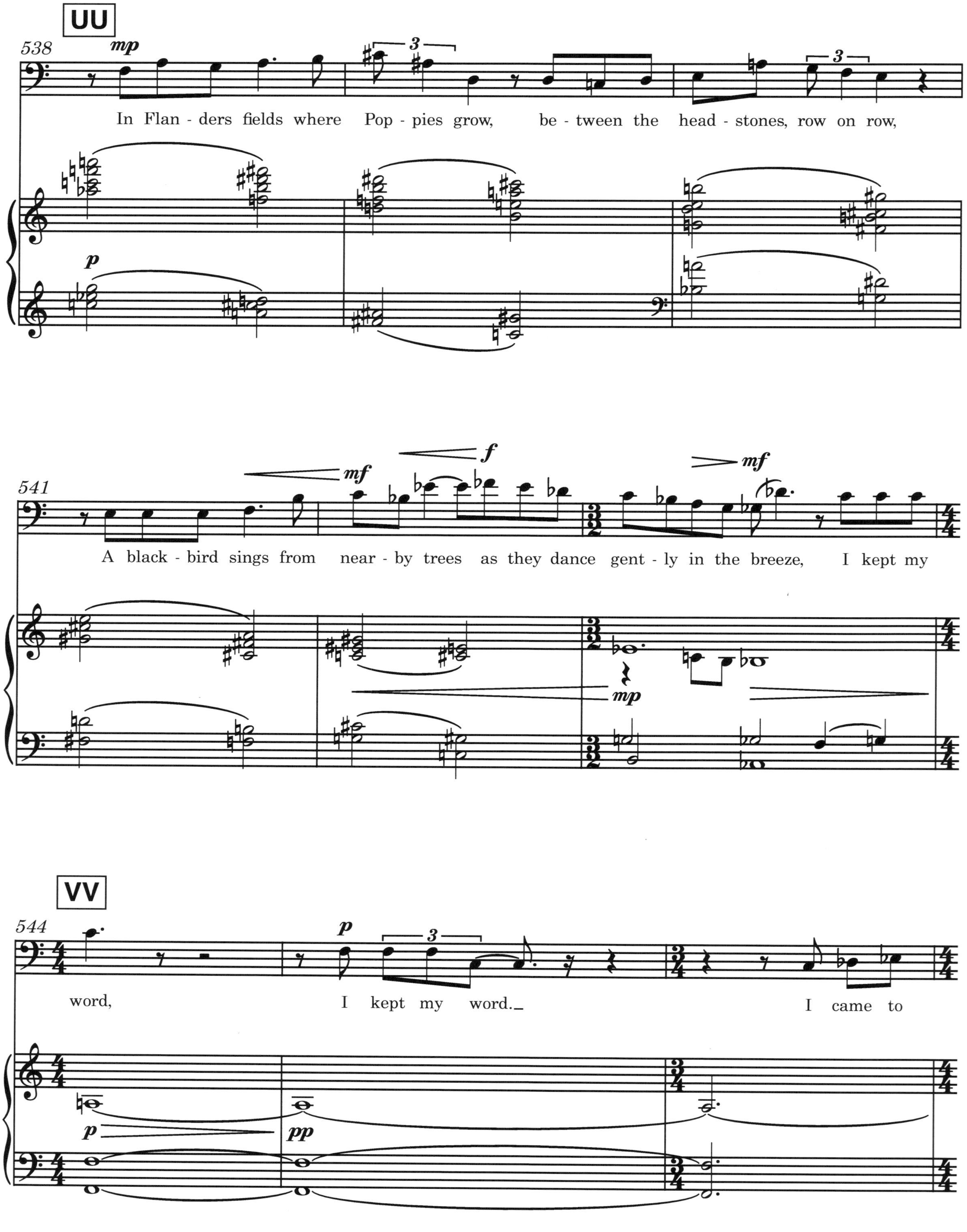
UU
538
mp
In Flan - ders fields where Pop - pies grow, be - tween the head - stones, row on row,
3
3
p
541
mf
f
mf
A black - bird sings from near - by trees as they dance gent - ly in the breeze, I kept my
mp
VV
544
p
word, I kept my word._ I came to
3
p
pp

54 Last Man Standing

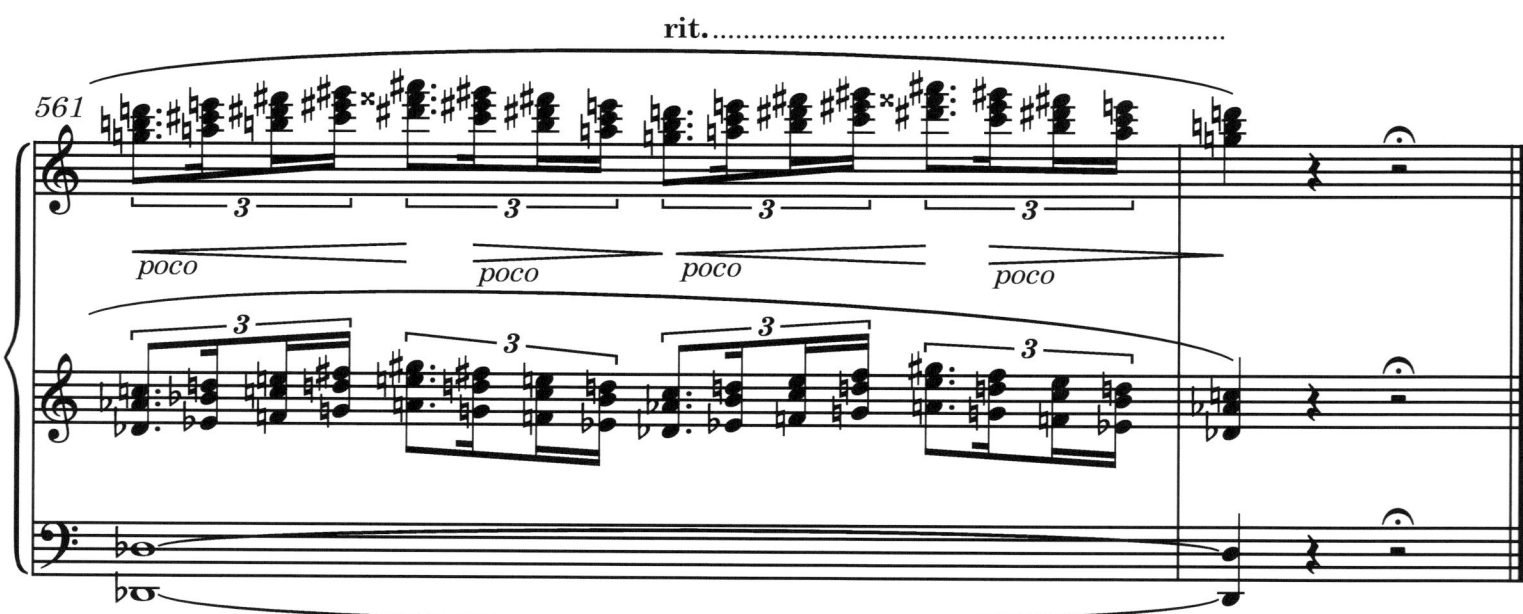